Outer gatehouse at Raby Castle

THE CASTLES
AND TOWER HOUSES
OF COUNTY DURHAM

Mike Salter

FOLLY PUBLICATIONS

ACKNOWLEDGEMENTS

Most of the photographs in this book were taken by the author, and a number of old postcards from his collection have also been reproduced. The author also drew the plans, sketches and the map. The plans are to common scales of 1:400 for towers and gatehouses, 1:800 for courtyard buildings, and 1:4000 and 1:10000 for site plans. Some of the plans are partly or wholly based on drawings which were amongst a considerable amount of material made available by Peter Ryder, who also provided much useful advice and helped with transport and accommodation. Thanks are also due to Helen Thomas for help with transport and support generally.

AUTHOR'S NOTES

This series of books (see full list inside back cover) are intended as portable field guides giving as much information and illustrative material as possible in volumes of modest size, weight and price. As a whole the series gives a lot of information on lesser known sites about which little information has tended to appear in print. The aim in the castle books has been to mention, where the information is known to the author, owners or custodians of buildings who erected or altered parts of them, and those who were the first or last to hold an estate, an important office, or a title. Those in occupation at the time of dramatic events such as sieges or royal visits are also often named. Other owners and occupants whose lives had little effect on the condition of the buildings are not generally mentions, nor are most 19th and 20th century events, unless particularly dramatic, nor ghost stories or legends.

The books are intended to be used in conjunction with the Ordnance Survey 1:50,000 maps. Grid references are given in the gazetteers together with a coding system indicating which buildings can be visited or easily seen by the public, which is explained on page 13. Generally speaking, maps will be required to find most of the lesser known sites, the majority of which are not normally open to the public.

Each level of a building is called a storey in this book, the basement being the first or lowest storey with its floor near courtyard level unless mentioned as otherwise.

Measurements given in the text and scales on the plans are given in metres, the unit used by the author for all measurements taken on site. Although the buildings were designed using feet and inches the metric scales are much easier to use and are now standard amongst those studying historic buildings and ancient sites. For those who feel a need to make a conversion 3 metres is almost 10 feet. Unless specifically mentioned as otherwise all dimensions are external at or near ground level, but above the plinth if there is one. On plans the original work is shown black, post-1800 work is stippled, and alterations and additions or intermediate periods are hatched.

ABOUT THE AUTHOR

Mike Salter is 48 and has been a professional writer and publisher since he went on the Government Enterprise Allowance Scheme for unemployed people in 1988. He is particularly interested in the planning and layout of medieval buildings and has a huge collection of plans of castles and churches he has measured during tours (mostly by bicycle and motorcycle) throughout all parts of the British Isles since 1968. Wolverhampton born and bred, Mike now lives in an old cottage beside the Malvern Hills. His other interests include walking, maps, railways, board games, morris dancing, playing percussion instruments and calling dances with a folk group.

First published July 2002. Copyright Mike Salter 2002.
Folly Publications, Folly Cottage, 151 West Malvern Rd, Malvern, Worcs WR14 4AY
Printed by Aspect Design, 89 Newtown Rd, Malvern, Worcs WR14 2PD

Lumley Castle

CONTENTS

A map of sites described appears inside the front cover.

INTRODUCTION

The story of castle building in County Durham begins with the invasion by William, Duke of Normandy in 1066. During his twenty year reign as king of England William I founded many castles including that at Durham itself in 1072. William gave estates to his chief followers in return for specified periods of military service, and the new lords gave units of land called manors to their knights, also in return for military service, which often included garrison duty. The system was known as feudalism and was an innovation in England. The thin veneer of landowning and French-speaking Normans thus consolidated their fragile hold over the Saxon populace by constructing castles serving as residences, strongholds and symbols of rank. The Romans, Saxons and Danes all built forts and defences around settlements but the Normans introduced the idea of powerful individuals erecting fortresses to serve as their private residences and as the administrative centres of groups of manors. In County Durham the position was unusual in that there was an additional threat from the Scots, and in the late 11th century the Scottish kings had a claim to adjoining Northumberland. In County Durham the Normans continued a system begun in the 10th century whereby the bishop also assumed the role of earl. In fact the county was made a palatinate under which military service was due to the bishop, who became a semi-independent ruler issuing his own coinage, and, in later years when castle building had to be authorised by a royal licence, such construction in County Durham was licensed by the bishop. Some of the powers of the palatinate were only recovered by the Crown in 1836.

The castle at Durham formed a common pattern for late 11th century castles in having a high mound raised from material taken out of a surrounding ditch, on top of which would be raised the lord's residence in the form of a two or three storey timber-framed tower surrounded by a palisade. The mound summit would be reached by a ramp up from a forecourt or bailey in which were sited a range of stores, workshops, a hall and other apartments, and a chapel, all originally built of wood, except that at Durham, the chapel, at least was a stone building from the start, or very shortly afterwards. Sometimes the mound took an alternative form known to modern writers as a ringwork, with a high rampart surrounding the lord's house, and the greater castles usually had an additional outer bailey beyond the main entrance. Castles of these types continued to be built for over a century after the Norman Conquest. Their basic design varied according to the terrain and the resouces available, and in any case most of them were modified over the years. Baileys and other outworks were omitted or duplicated and made whatever size and shape local circumstances dictated. Natural landscape features were used where possible, hillocks and spurs being shaped and heightened into steep sides and level-topped mottes, whilst castles on low ground were often protected by water-filled moats.

The motte at Bishopton

Brancepeth Castle

Buildings of mortared stone needed several years of peaceful conditions for their construction because they would have been vulnerable during long periods when foundations were being laid, so initially structures raised on timber posts and earth ramparts were seen as an easy, quick option. Timber buildings were vulnerable to accidental or deliberate destruction by fire and eventually rotted away when in constant contact with damp soil. Although timber-framed buildings remained an important part of many castles throughout the medieval period, the main defences and the chief buildings they enclosed were eventually rebuilt in stone. Durham may have had stone defences by 1100, and there were stone walls at Barnard Castle by the late 12th century. At Durham a stone shell wall (rebuilt in the 14th century and again in the 19th) replaced the palisade on the motte summit. The pre-13th century parts there also include a rectangular gatehouse, and a hall block and other parts. Barnard also has a rectangular gatehouse and remains of a Norman solar block, behind which a round tower or keep containing additional private rooms was added in the early 13th century. Work of the 13th century is otherwise not common amongst the castles of County Durham. Bishop Bek's hall of the 1280s remains at Durham, although the circuit of walls and towers that he added at Bishop Auckland has almost vanished. The hall at Bishop Auckland is partly his work, partly late 12th century, and partly of the 1660s, when it became a chapel.

Durham Castle from the west

Hylton Castle   Witton Castle

County Durham contains an important group of late 14th century castles. The licences to crenellate that survive for two of them help with dating, work at Raby being authorised in 1378, and work at Lumley being authorised by the bishop in 1389 and by the king in 1392. The work at Raby was only a remodelling and strengthening of an existing early to mid 14th century building by John Neville, and his other castle at Brancepeth was also a rebuilding of an older structure. Whilst Lumley has a regular layout with four ranges around a court, four corner towers, and gatehouse flanked by square turrets in the middle of one side, Raby and Brancepeth have much more irregular layouts, although that at Raby was slightly more regular before the additions of the 1370s. Brancepeth had a large enclosure with towers set at intervals, one close-set group containing the main rooms. The towers of all three castles are large and rectangular and those at Brancepeth and Lumley have diagonally projecting corner turrets with tops that are machicolated at the sides. Turrets with machicolations also appeared on two corners and as a pair flanking a gateway on a building of the 1390s at Hylton, although the other two corners had circular bartizans of a type more common in Scotland. Of an earlier 14th century courtyard castle at Ravensworth there only remain two of the four corner towers. Of the prior of Durham's camera or solar block at Muggleswick one end wall stands high with corner turrets with corbelled parapets, and parts of the domestic buildings at Barnard Castle and Durham Castle (where Bishop Hatfield extended the great hall) are also 14th century work. The lost castle of Stockton had a southern English plan with round corner towers and square intermediate ones. The older motte and bailey sites that had not been refortified in stone had probably been abandoned by this period.

Witton Castle, licensed in 1410, has an altered tower house and a nearly complete barmkin or walled court. The barmkin wall has several bartizans and the tower has four turrets, two of them projecting diagonally. Bradley Hall, licensed in 1431, has lost its curtain wall and only a series of vaulted cellars remain of the main building, which seems to have had an upper hall and solar end-to-end. This site was protected by a wet moat, as was Holmside Hall, where fragments of a curtain wall and a range remain. Holmside is best classed as a stronghouse or fortified manor house, and the ruins at Hollinside and Langley also belonged to this type, Langley being as late as the early 16th century. Of other late medieval fortified houses there remain moats or traces of them at Low Dinsdale, Low Butterby, and Sockburn, which was licensed in 1470. Many medieval manor houses were provided with moats and they remained in fashion until the 16th century. Moats did not require licences and a distinction between buildings that were fortified and those that were not is not easy to make. A change of status from house to castle or from castle to unfortified house was not unknown. Water filled ditches were not necessarily military in purpose. A moat was a permanent and efficient boundary for keeping vagrants, wild animals and malefactors out of manorial enclosures, and would have also been useful to control the comings and goings of domestic animals, servants and members of the family. At all periods moats were appreciated as scenic features, and served as a habitat for fish, eels and water fowl, although separate fishponds were often provided.

Other tower houses in the county which defy close dating are at Dawdon, Hunstanworth, Ludworth, and the Old Lodge in Raby Park. There are no remains of two towers which formed rectories at Houghton-le-Spring and Redmarshall, licensed in 1483 and 1462 respectively, nor does anything remain of the great north gate of Durham city wall as rebuilt in the early 15th century. At Durham there is a second chapel and a gallery added by Bishop Tunstall in the 1530s and Bishop Auckland has a range of that period, and Walworth a round tower with a gunport, but 16th century work is generally sparse amongst the castles. Of the second half of the century there are a few windows and some heraldry in the courtyard at Lumley.

The western hall from the courtyard at Durham

In the medieval period castle walls of rubble were sometimes limewashed outside, making them look very different to the way they appear today. Ashlar-work and dressed stones around windows and doorways would be left uncovered. Domestic rooms would have had whitewashed walls decorated with murals of biblical, historical or heroic scenes mostly painted in red, yellow and black. By the 14th century wall hangings decorated with the same themes came into fashion. Although used in churches, glass was expensive and uncommon in secular buildings before the late medieval period, so windows were originally closed with shutters. As a result rooms were dark when the weather was too cold or wet for the shutters to be opened for ventilation. In the later medieval period large openings in the outer walls often had iron bars or grilles protecting them, even if high off the ground. Living rooms usually had fireplaces, although some halls had central hearths with the smoke escaping through louvres in the roof. Latrines are commonly provided in the thickness of the walls or in projecting turrets and help to indicate which rooms were intended for living or sleeping in, rather than just storage space. There was little privacy in the early castles but by the late 14th century the buildings contained individual rooms for large numbers of people, although those of low rank still lacked much privacy.

Furnishings were quite sparse up until the 15th century, and the embrasures of upper storey windows often have built-in seats. Lords with several castles and houses tended to circulate around them administering their manorial courts and consuming agricultural produce on the spot. They might also be away at court or on military or diplomatic service. Their wives or junior family members might be left in residence but often castles were left almost empty for long periods, gradually crumbling away with only a skeleton staff to administer estates. However, the castles of County Durham suffered less from this than other areas and in the late medieval period Barnard was the only major castle with a permanently absent lord.

The bastle or pele at Baal Hill House

Old Print of Raby Castle

The Civil War of the 1640s did not seriously affect the castles of County Durham except for the dismantling of the outer walls at Bishop Auckland and Stockton. In the 1660s the domestic buildings at Bishop Auckland were patched up and the medieval hall turned into a chapel. There is not much evidence left of work of the same period at Raby which was mostly swept away by further campaigns in the 18th and 19th centuries. The major castles have fared better than those of most counties. Bishop Auckland and Raby are still lordly residence, and Brancepeth as rebuilt in the 19th century, and Lumley as modified in the early 18th century have also remained occupied together with Witton Castle and the Old Lodge in Raby Park. A new house built in the 18th century at Ravensworth has not survived and the medieval towers lie derelict, whilst the much altered building at Streatlam was demolished in the 1920s. Of the ruined sites Barnard and Ludworth are maintained in state care, as is Hylton, which was remodelled and remained in use up until the late 19th century.

The Chapel Tower at Raby

GAZETTEER OF CASTLES IN COUNTY DURHAM

ARCHDEACON NEWTON   NZ 254172   V

Of a moated house of the Archdeacon of Durham there remains a much altered 14th century building which is thought to have been a service wing to a hall lying east of it. The jambs of arches at each end of the east side may be relics of porches at each end of the screens passage of the hall. Traces of a moat survived until the 1960s.

BAAL HILL HOUSE   NZ 074385

This farmhouse high above Wolsingham is thought to have been occupied by the bailiff of a park here. It measures 14m by 8.2m over walls 1.2m thick and has a vaulted basement which is divided in two with an original doorway at each end. The second storey was divided into a living room with a smaller room at the east end, into which there is an upper entrance, there being no stair between these levels. The third storey replacing attic sleeping lofts appears to be of 1894. See bastles list, page 63.

BARNARD CASTLE   NZ 049165   E

The castle here was founded by Guy de Balliol, granted the estate by William II in 1095. It takes its name from Guy's nephew Bernard, who succeeded him in 1125. Bernard and his sons Guy, d1162, and Bernard, d1199, enlarged the castle and rebuilt it in stone. It then passed to Eustace de Helicourt, who took the name Balliol, although the Bishop of Durham had possession as security for a debt, and probably held it until 1212, when King John ordered the castle to be returned to Eustace's son Hugh. In July 1216 the castle was besieged by Alexander II of Scotland in support of the barons rebelling against King John. It seems to have remained untaken, and one of the rebel barons, Eustace de Vesci, was killed by a crossbow bolt during the attack. The Round Tower seems to have been added around this time. Hugh's son, John de Balliol married a Scottish heiress, Devorguilla of Galloway, although the incarceration of her illegitimate brother Thomas in the castle for over sixty years was necessary to ensure the de Balliol hold on her lands. In 1264 the castle was handed over to barons loyal to Simon de Montfort after John de Balliol was captured at the battle of Lewes. In 1278 John was succeeded by his son John who in 1290 became a contender for the Scottish throne. The issue was decided in his favour by Edward I of England but in 1296 John Balliol rejected Edward I's overlordship and was deposed. After a period of imprisonment in the Tower of London he retired to his estates in Picardy in France, his English and Scottish estates having been forfeited.

Barnard Castle

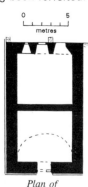

0   5
metres

Plan of
Baal Hill House

The gateway of the Town Ward at Barnard Castle

The bishops of Durham had an ancient claim to the estate and from 1296 until 1306 Bishop Anthony Bek had possession of the castle. Shortly before his death in 1307, Edward I granted the castle to Guy de Beauchamp, Earl of Warwick, and his heirs held the castle until 1449. The Beauchamps were absentee lords since they lived at Warwick Castle when not busy serving in the royal army, and although the inner and middle wards were maintained the other two wards and their buildings became superfluous and were allowed to decay. The castle then passed to Richard Neville, who became Earl of Warwick, and was married to Anne, daughter of Richard Beauchamp, who had died in 1439. Richard became known as "Warwick the Kingmaker" since he was instrumental in putting Edward IV on the throne in 1461, but then turned against him and reinstated Henry IV. After his death at the battle of Barnet in 1471 the Bishop of Durham again claimed the castle but it was granted by Edward IV to his younger brother the Duke of Gloucester. He became king as Richard III in 1483 and intended to remodel the castle, but little was done before his defeat and death at Bosworth in 1485. Henry VII returned the castle to Warwick's widow Anne but she surrendered it back to the king on condition it was returned to her successors. In practice the Crown had possession of the decayed castle until 1603.

The castle was captured during the Pilgrimage of Grace in 1536, mainly because constable Robert Bowes was unable to trust his garrison, since they sympathised with the rebels. At the start of the rebellion of the earls of Westmorland and Northumberland in 1569 the castle was provisioned and garrisoned by Sir George Bowes. When the castle was attacked by 5000 rebels early in December Sir George found himself in a similar situation as his ancestor in 1536. After the outer ward was breached and captured, and then the town ward also fell, the garrison's water supply was cut off and many of the defenders then defected by jumping over the walls, 35 of them suffering death or injury as a result. Sir George then surrendered on terms, but the fortnight spent in capturing the castle had given the Earl of Sussex, Lord President of the North, the time he need to assemble a force to crush the rebellion.

The inner ward wall at Barnard Castle

In 1574 a survey recorded the castle as being in a decayed condition. It was granted by James I in 1603 to Robert Carr, whom he made Earl of Somerset, but upon his disgrace in 1615 it went to the Prince of Wales. The prince sold the castle to the City of London in 1626 and in 1630 it was resold to Sir Henry Vane. None of these owners used the decaying castle and Sir Henry took material from it for building works at Raby. Before long the place had been reduced to its present condition. In the early 19th century the Round Tower was occupied by an eccentric squatter who dressed as a monk. The outer ward remains in private hands and is not open to the public but the other three wards were placed in State care in 1952 by Lord Barnard of Raby, and they are now administered by English Heritage.

The gateway of the Town Ward at Barnard Castle

Middle gatehouse at Barnard Castle   *The round tower at Barnard Castle*

Barnard Castle is placed on a rocky platform high above the east side of the Tees. It consists of an inner ward 42m across on the site of the original ringwork, a middle ward of similar size SE of it, the town ward to the east and the outer ward to the south. These last two wards were spacious and resulted in a walled area 290m long by 110m wide, making one of the largest non-royal castles in Britain. Little remains of the thin, towerless wall of the outer ward and its east-facing gatehouse and the nearby chapel of St Margaret SW of it have been destroyed along with all the internal buildings. This part of the castle is not open to the public.

The town ward is more complete, although parts of the east wall (in which was a postern) are missing and there are only traces of some of the southernmost internal buildings. The Brackenbury Tower measuring 13m by 8m on the east contained two storeys of lodgings, the lower level being vaulted and the upper level reached by an external stair being for a household official. On the north side is a gatehouse containing rooms for a porter and guard either side of a passage with a round arch of two orders with a bead moulding on the imposts, with further rooms above. The gateway is flanked by a solid round turret. Further west the curtain wall changes alignment at a square tower containing a dovecote. Between here and the Round Tower is a postern with a portcullis groove in the bottom of the inner ward ditch.

Half of the internal space of the middle ward was taken up by the rock-cut ditch which protected the two weakest sides of the inner ward. It is thought that part of the remainder was taken up with stables. The middle ward had gates facing both the town ward and outer ward and controlled the only means of communication between them. The gatehouse facing the outer ward was a substantial structure 14m square with rooms flanking a central passage, but only the lower parts of its west side remain and the whole south side of the middle ward has vanished. The chambers above the middle gate were used by the constable of the castle.

The inner ward is protected by a 12th century curtain wall 2.3m thick around its east and south sides. The small polygonal turret containing a postern on the NE and the Prison Tower on the east, also polygonal, are late 14th or 15th century, although the latter replaces an older structure. The curtain between them has original pilaster buttresses and faces a level berm between it and the ditch. Backing onto this wall are foundations of a bakehouse with a cistern or cold store. The original early 12th century gatehouse was superseded a few years later by a new gateway immediately east of it, and in the 14th century a new approach was made, so that one crossed a bridge adjacent to the cliff edge, then turned east within a barbican, and then turned north again within a D-shaped bastion built in front of the new gateway. The old gateway then became the residential Headlam Tower, and c1200 was extended 3m out to the edge of the cliff to the SW. North of here the curtain wall is replaced by a thin modern parapet. Here lay the kitchen and service rooms with apartments above. Of the principal rooms ranged around the NW corner only the high outer walls perched on the cliff edge and foundations facing the court remain. The 13th century hall was quite modestly sized at 13m by 9m. The two surviving windows facing the river are 14th century. South of it lay the 14th and 15th century Mortham Tower with in its lowest stage the main service passage flanked by a pantry and buttery.

North of the hall was the 12th century great chamber 21m long but only 6m wide, set over a basement used for storage or offices. The great chamber has a fine 15th century oriel window overlooking the river. In the early 13th century it was supplemented by several extra chambers in a round tower 11.4m in diameter over walls 2.6m thick added on the north side. This tower originally rose about 22m from its battered base outside the castle to the top of the lost parapet, and is faced with sandstone ashlar. The first two levels have fireplaces and latrines but were lighted only by narrow loops, the lowest being dome vaulted. Access between these rooms by straight stairs through a rectangular vaulted chamber on the SE side, where the round is made into a square corner to fit against the great chamber block. A stair within the curve of the wall then rose to the upper levels. The third storey was later given large rectangular windows, although it lacks a fireplace or latrine.

Plans of Barnard Castle

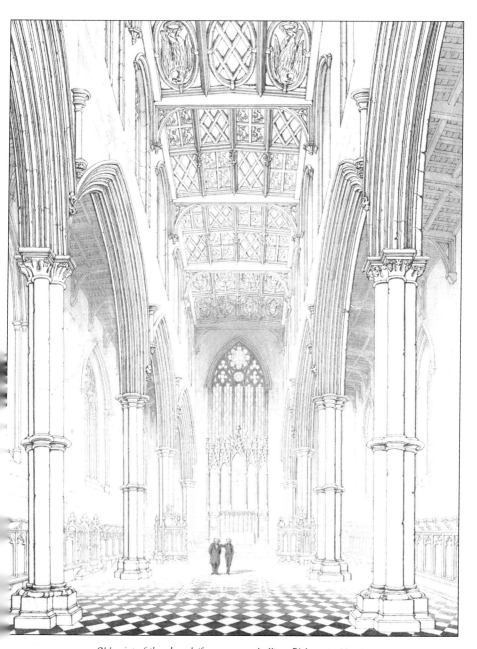

Old print of the chapel (former great hall) at Bishop Auckland

The palace at Bishop Auckland

BISHOP AUCKLAND CASTLE   NZ 215301   O

Now the only residence of the Bishop of Durham, this palace on a promontory at the north end of the town existed by the 1150s. It is first referred to as a castle in 1346 and on the basis of Leland's description of c1540 it is thought that Bishop Anthony Bek (1284-1311) built a curtain wall with round and rectangular flanking towers. The palace is described in 1634 as "of great strength, compassed with a thick stone wall". The only possible relics of it are the low retaining wall on the north side with a round projection, possibly the remains of a turret. The 5m by 6.5m embattled tower standing 6.5m high in a derelict and somewhat altered condition on the west side is medieval but is more likely to be late 14th or 15th century in its present form.

Charles I stayed in the palace on his way up to Scotland in 1633 and he was brought back to it as a prisoner with the Scottish army in 1647. Later that year the palace was sold for £6100 to Sir Arthur Hazlerigg, who is known to have demolished quite a lot of it (and probably all the defences) to build a new block. At the Restoration the palace was recovered by Bishop John Cosin (1660-72), who then demolished Hazlerigg's block and renovated the medieval buildings. A fine aisled hall thought to have been built by Bishop Hugh de Puiset in the late 12th century was then made into a chapel of St Peter. The south side was refaced in ashlar with alternate stones with either rectangles or diamonds standing out in relief. The five light east window, the clerestory and the fine furnishings are also of the 1660s. The lower windows and the pointed arches of the arcades are the work of Bishop Bek c1300 but the quatrefoil arcade piers with waterleaf capitals are original Late Norman work. When the building was a hall it had kitchens at the east end, where there are now just steps facing the gardens. The dais was at the west end, where there is now a porch erected in 1794-6 by Bishop Barrington serving both the chapel and the residence lying SW of it. The screen wall south of the buildings is also of that period.

The palace at Bishop Auckland

The south range has a bay window upon which appear the arms of Bishop Ruthall (1509-23) and Bishop Tunstall (1530-61). This part has work of their period, as does the narrow range known as Scotland which projects to the west and contains a long gallery on the upper storey. On the south side of the original south wing is a block added by Bishop Trevor (1752-71), who carried out much work on the buildings, which 1737 were described as "very much out of repair". The east range also contains medieval and early 16th century work but the present layout and decoration of the rooms is mostly the work of Bishop Cosin, Bishop Trevor and Bishop Barrington. The outer gateway standing near the site of a gatehouse built by Bishop Walter Skirlaw (1388-1406) was also the work of Bishop Trevor. When Bishop Cosin made the old hall into a chapel he also adapted the presence chamber near the north end of the east range into a new hall. There is little to show for the £3000 spent upon "repairing and ornamenting" the building by Bishop Neile (1617-28).

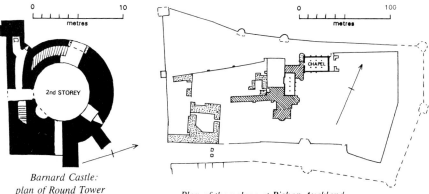

Barnard Castle: plan of Round Tower

Plan of the palace at Bishop Auckland

Bradley Hall

BISHOP MIDDLEHAM CASTLE   NZ 328311

The bishops of Durham probably had a house here in the late 11th century, although the first mention of it is not until 1146. A new hall, kitchen and chapel were built in the 1320s, and considerable repairs were carried out in 1349, but in 1384 the house was said to be worth nothing probably because it was then already in a poor state of repair. A survey of 1647 describes the house as "totally demolished" except for a barn and granary in good repair. The site was sold to Thomas Haslerigg two years later. An underground passage is mentioned in the late 18th century and foundations of a square tower are referred to in 1823. The site lies near the church south of the village, and occupies the SE end of a promontory with steep drops to the east and south, although there is no trace of a ditch on the other sides. Banks indicate an enclosure 60m by 20m with an outer enclosure 25m by 9m at the SW corner. There are footings of one wall 1m thick and traces of others under the grass.

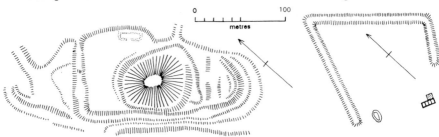

Plan of Bishopton Castle

Bradley Hall: site plan

BISHOPTON CASTLE   NZ 367209   F

This castle was protected by marshland and is assumed to have been built early in the 12th century by Roger de Conyers after he was granted an estate here by Bishop Ranulf Flambard. It consisted of an oval motte rising 12m to a summit 15m by 9m set within an oval bailey 220m long by 85m wide, but excavations have found evidence of a remodelling in 1143, when new ditches were dug at the north and south ends, the latter considerably shortening the main space of the bailey north of the mound. In that year the castle was successfully held against an attack by the would-be bishop William Comyn. The Conyers family later transferred to Sockburn.

BRADLEY HALL   NZ 108362   V

This estate was originally held by a family who took their name from it. By 1345 it had passed to the Eure family, and in 1431 Sir William Eure obtained a licence to crenellate his house here from Bishop Thomas Langley. They subsequently fell out and Eure later threatened the bishop's life. From this period must date the ruined building 30.6m by 10m containing four vaulted cellars each with doorways with four-centred heads, above which was a hall and at least one chamber. The 18th century farmhouse adjoining the NE corner may be a much rebuilt range added to provide extra private rooms. These buildings lie in the southern corner of a platform 155m by 115m the NW and NE sides of which still have partly water-filled ditches and ramparts up to 2m high. An account written in 1804 suggests that this enclosure had a stone wall with round turrets or towers at some of the corners, but this may not have been added until the hall was rebuilt by Sir George Bowes, who was granted Bradley after it was confiscated from Robert Tempest after the 1569 rebellion.

0   10
|_|_|_|_|_|_____|
        metres

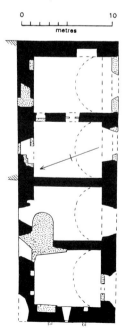

Plan of Bradley Hall   *Bradley Hall*

BRANCEPETH CASTLE   NZ 222378   V

The Bulmer Tower on the west side is named after a family who are thought to have had a motte and bailey castle on this site which passed by marriage to Geoffrey de Neville c1175. The castle is first mentioned in 1216 when Henry de Neville was pardoned for rebellion. The motte probably disappeared when the castle was rebuilt in the 1360s or 70s by John Neville. His son Ralph, who succeeded in 1389, was created Earl of Westmorland by Richard II in 1397, by which time the castle must have assumed its final medieval form. The castle may have been abandoned after the forfeiture of Charles, 6th Earl for his part in the rebellion of 1569. The decayed building had a succession of absentee landlords in the early 17th century, and it may have suffered some damage during the Civil War, when it was confiscated by Parliament from Ralph Cole. The Coles recovered the castle in the 1660s but in 1701 conveyed it to Sir Henry Belasyse. His descendant the Earl of Fauconberg sold the castle in 1776 to John Tempest and twenty years later it was sold again to the Sunderland banker, William Russell. The fortune he made out of coal enabled his son Matthew to commence a thorough rebuilding. In 1850 the castle passed by marriage to Gustavus Hamilton, 7th Viscount Boyne, who employed Anthony Salvin to do further works which cost about £250,000. The castle was abandoned by the 9th Viscount in 1922 and left to decay until 1939 when it became the headquarters of the Durham Light Infantry for over two decades. It was later used as a laboratory by a glass company and it is now occupied by various small businesses and tenants.

The link block at Brancepeth

The Neville Tower at Brancepeth

The northern curtain wall at Brancepeth.

The Westmorland Tower at Brancepeth

Constable's Tower at Brancepeth

The Bulmer Tower at Brancepeth

The castle is an extremely impressive building with a court 70m across, although much of it dates from the two 19th century remodellings. The curtain wall on the north side looks like a 13th century structure heightened and provided with angle turrets in the 1360s or 70s. The other 14th century parts are large rectangular towers grouped around the SE and SW sides. The towers have vaulted basements and vary slightly in size but they average 17m by 9m and project almost entirely beyond the earlier curtain. They all have three storeys with set-offs marking the floor levels and are characterised by diagonal corner buttresses carried up as small turrets. The west-facing Bulmer Tower and the south-facing Neville Tower contain rib-vaulted high status chambers on the second storey and are connected by a block similar in design to the towers themselves but evidently slightly later. This group almost certainly replaced the motte. The rib-vaulted chamber in the linking block was probably a withdrawing room giving access to the private apartments in the Neville Tower from the main hall in the Bulmer Tower. There must have been service rooms further north where there is now a wide 19th century block replacing a 16th century range. The servants' hall in the basement of the Bulmer Tower has a fireplace, and end loop connecting with corner mural chambers (one of which has access to a latrine) and four other loops, one of which was later broken out to give access to the link block basement. The latter has a blocked service staircase. The Neville Tower and the Constable's Tower further east have their end walls built much thinner than the side walls carrying the thrust of the vaults. Apart from small loops, most of them blocked, the only ancient windows are one each of the 15th and 17th century in the Neville Tower. The east facing Westmorland Tower was mostly rebuilt in the 1860s to contain a two storey chapel. It then gained new machicolated parapets on the north and south sides. The original NE gatehouse with square turrets facing the field and an off-centre entrance portal has been replaced by a larger neo-Norman structure of great projection and with circular turrets. The Russell Tower in the middle of the south front is entirely 19th century but there was a medieval turret in this position.

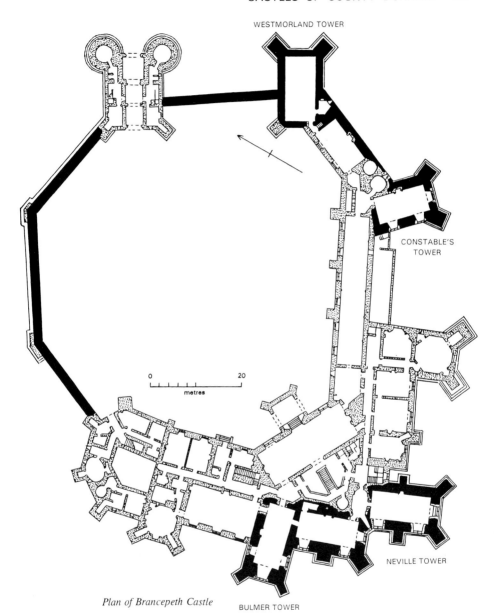

Plan of Brancepeth Castle

WESTMORLAND TOWER

CONSTABLE'S TOWER

NEVILLE TOWER

BULMER TOWER

0   20
metres

CLEADON TOWER NZ 385624

The oldest parts of the present building are mid 16th century. The doorway and four fireplaces have four-centred arches and the arms of the Chambers family appear on one fireplace. Until c1800 a medieval solar tower was attached to the building.

COTHERSTONE CASTLE   NZ 013199   V

The castle built c1090 by Bodin, brother of Earl Alan of Richmond, comprised a motte rising 4m to a summit 30m across with a kidney-shaped bailey platform 35m across to the SW and probably also a larger outer bailey delineated by the present farm track around the south and east sides of the site, which has a steep drop on the west and north sides to the confluence of the Tees and Balder rivers. The castle later passed to Henry Fitz-Hervey, and the fragments of walling up to 1.2m thick on the west and north sides of the motte summit are assumed to date from 1201 when he was licensed to crenellate his residence here. The castle then passed to the Fitz-Hughs and is thought to have been captured and destroyed by the Scots in 1316. In the middle of the outer bailey is the site of a well which was used until recently. This site lay in Yorkshire prior to the 1974 boundary changes.

COWPEN BEWLEY: LOW GRANGE   NZ 471255

A medieval building at Low Grange belonging to the Priors of Durham, which was removed prior to the construction of a new housing estate, was found by excavation to overlie at its SW corner the foundations of an older building 9.6m wide over walls 1.6m thick with pilaster buttresses set in the middle and clasping the corners of the east wall. The building was correctly orientated for a chapel but seems to have been massive enough to have been an embattled solar block or tower house, perhaps of 13th century date.

Dawdon: recess

Dawdon Tower

Dawton Tower

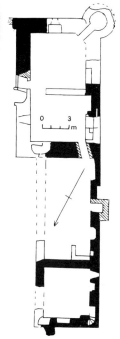

Plan of Dawdon Tower

DARLINGTON CASTLE   NZ 274130

A mound in woodland by the suburb of Blackwell rises 8m above the River Tees. This is probably the site of the "tenement called the Castle Hill" which is mentioned in a 14th century document, and mostly destroyed by flooding in 1771.

DAWDON TOWER   NZ 418485   F

In an oddly low-lying site in the bottom of a narrow valley SW of Seaham are ruins of tower 14.8m by 9.3m long over walls 1.6m thick. A passage in the NE wall probably led through to a hall block, and until fairly recently part of a gatehouse stood further east, so a walled court is likely to have existed. The tower basement seems to have been a living room since there is a fireplace in the SW wall and adjoining it and also in the SE wall are remains of window embrasures fitted with seats. Only the footings remain of a 3.6m diameter round tower at the south corner. This was probably added in the 16th century and the crosswall abutting against the fireplace may also have been inserted then. Little remains of the upper levels except for a fine mid 14th century ogival-headed lavabo or buffet recess in the east corner, probably reset. In the west corner a doorway has been broken through towards a range 7m wide extending for 18m towards the slope of the valley side. The is no conclusive evidence for the date of the range, which contained three basement rooms, perhaps with vaults and has a service staircase in the north corner towards what were probably grander rooms on the vanished upper level. A fireplace remains on the SW side, south of which there has been some rebuilding. The tower probably existed by 1375 when Sir Jordan de Dawdon obtained a licence from the prior and convent of Durham for a private oratory in his manor house here.

DURHAM CASTLE   NZ 275423   O

Waltheof, the newly created Earl of Northumberland, is thought to have founded this castle in 1072 on the orders of William I. He was executed in 1076 after being implicated in a rebellion, and the earldom of Northumberland was then placed in the hands of Walcher, who had been appointed Bishop of Durham in 1071. The castle seems to have been intended from the outset to be his seat as ruler (bishop and earl) of the palatinate of Durham. Walcher was murdered at Gateshead in 1080 and was succeeded by William de St Carilef. He fled in exile after rebelling against William II in 1088 but returned in 1091 to begin work on rebuilding the cathedral. By the time Ranulph Flambard was made bishop in 1099 the castle seems to have had at least some stone buildings and the east end and crossing of the cathedral had been completed. Flambard completed the nave of the cathedral and built a stone wall to replace the palisade round the peninsular on which both buildings. In 1140 the bishopric was usurped by William Comyn, and not until 1144 did he relinquish his claim in favour of a new bishop, William de St Barbara. In 1143 the city was blockaded by Comyn, who converted the churchyard of St Giles church 1km ENE of the castle into a siege-castle overlooking the city. A description of the castle written by Prior Laurence about this time suggests that the motte was then surmounted by a stone shell wall with a timber tower inside it supported on four stout corner posts.

Many of the bailey buildings were rebuilt by Bishop Hugh de Puiset (1153-95) after they were damaged by a fire which swept through the city. The Elvet Bridge on the east side of the city was also built at this time. After the rebellion of 1174 Henry II took possession of the castle because of the bishop's doubtful loyalty but on Richard I's accession in 1189 the castle was returned to the bishop, who additionally held the earldom of Northumberland. The new watch tower and portcullis provided in 1211-12 when the vacant bishopric was in King John's hands, may have been elsewhere on the peninsular, the whole of which was often regarded in medieval times as "the castle".

The keep of Durham Castle

Norman Gallery at Durham   *Durham Castle*

Bishop Anthony Bek (1283-1311) was a noted builder of castles and at Durham he built a large new hall on the west side of the bailey. Bishop Thomas Hatfield (1345-81) rebuilt the keep and added a block at the south end of the west hall. Bishop Richard Fox (1494-1501) remodelled the kitchen and other parts which had fallen into decay in the 1480s, and Bishop Cuthbert Tunstall (1530-59) added a gallery in front of the north range, extending to a chapel he added in front of an older chapel. The castle was captured by the rebels during the rising of the northern earls in 1569. Little remains of the modifications made by Bishop Richard Neile (1617-28), partly because the castle was occupied by the Scottish army during the Civil War and they "spoiled and ruined it with gunpowder", after which it was sold off by the Commonwealth government to a Lord Mayor of London, mainly for the value of its materials. Bishop John Cosin, appointed after the Restoration of Charles II in 1660, found his castles at Auckland and Durham in ruins and spent large sums on rebuilding them. At Durham he renovated the apartments, demolished what remained of the barbican in front of the gatehouse and also filled in the ditch on that side. Further modifications were carried out by Bishop Crewe (1674-1722) and Bishop Trevor (1752-71). The keep seems to have remained a ruin and the upper parts of it were demolished during the time of Bishop Thomas Thurlow (1787-91). Bishop Van Mildert was the last to hold the see as a palatinate, combining the offices of earl and bishop. The later bishops have had just a single residence at Bishop Auckland and the castle at Durham was handed over in 1840 to the university founded eight years earlier. It is still occupied as a college and students live in apartments in the keep.

The combined castle, cathedral precinct and walled town of Durham have a wonderfully strong and scenic site without equal in Britain. They are set upon a 600m long and 250m wide promontory rising up to 25m above a loop of the River Wear with the castle closing off most of the 200m wide neck of the promontory at the north end. The wedge-shaped castle bailey is 65m wide and extends from 90m from the west, where a hall block overhangs a steep drop to the river, to a polygonal keep on a motte at the eastern point of the site. The cathedral lies in the middle of the promontory with its western galilee chapel also overhanging the drop to the river. There was a well, accessible from above, between the 15th century buttresses of the galilee. The promontory probably had a palisade from when a cathedral was first established here at the end of the 10th century. Most of the circuit of walls which replaced the palisade still remain at least in part except for a 160m gap on the east, south of St Mary Le Bow Church, and a shorter gap on the west just north of the cathedral. The walls have been much rebuilt and replaced over the years and no original parapets remain. A few buttresses have been added, and some formed turrets, but there are no proper towers. The Water Gate at the SW corner and the Prebends Bridge it leads to are of the 1770s and replace an original gateway and bridge further south. Underneath the monastic guest house there is a postern leading to a long tunnel known as the Dark Entry, and there is another postern known as Windy Gap opening onto Palace Green north of the cathedral.

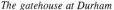

The gatehouse at Durham

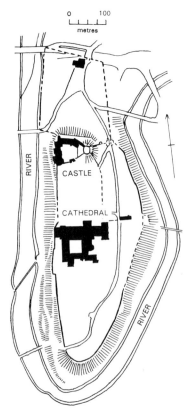

Durham: site plan

Durham: Water Gate in the city wall

St Mary Le Bow church marks the site of a crosswall between the NE corner of the cathedral and the vanished King's Gate leading to a lost medieval bridge just north of the present Bow Bridge. A gateway (hence the bow part of the name) under part of the church collapsed in 1635 and the damage to the church then caused was not made good until the 1670s. There was once another crosswall leading round from the castle keep to the NE corner of the cathedral to close off Palace Green. Apart from the main ward of the castle and the monastic precinct south of the cathedral the promontory was thus divided into three enclosures. On the north side a short length of wall ran past an early 14th century D-shaped bastion 9m in diameter (the base of which can bee seen through a grille near the end of Saddler Street) to the North Gate. This was by far the most important gateway and was provided with a new barbican flanking the drawbridge in the 1320s. In the 1420s Bishop Langley rebuilt the structure so that it could house prisoners that had formerly been kept in a prison on Palace Green. It long retained this function and a new exercise yard was created on the east side in a remodelling in 1773, but it was finally demolished in 1820 after completion of the existing Durham Prison. The building had a central passage flanked by towers which were square below but polygonal to the field above. There was a square adjunct on the west side and a polygonal SE stair-turret. The barbican also had turrets which were polygons rising from square bases. The former open space of the barbican was in the late 15th century filled by a wing built over it.

The walled promontory was largely reserved for officials, clergy, servants and retainers serving the castle, cathedral and monastic complex, and the market place lay outside the north end of the 12th century walled area. As a response to the threat of Scottish raids this area in turn was walled c1315-25 creating another enclosure 200m long by 180m wide. Little remains of this circuit except for a section of walling along the bank of the river on the west side. A gate at the SW corner at the head of the Framwell Bridge (originally built in the early 12th century) was demolished in 1760. There was another gate on the east side, facing Elvet Bridge, and on the north side, just NE of St Nicholas' church, lay the Clayport Gate, which was removed in 1791, although it had lost its upper chamber some time beforehand. Part of the Walkergate postern at the NW corner survived until 1960, when a new road was built across the site. This gateway was used in the 16th century by the Earl of Westmorland, who had a house called New Place in this corner of the city.

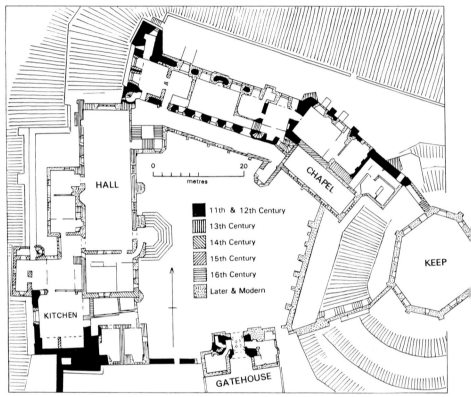

11th & 12th Century

13th Century

14th Century

15th Century

16th Century

Later & Modern

HALL

CHAPEL

KEEP

KITCHEN

GATEHOUSE

Plan of Durham Castle

The castle gatehouse is mid 12th century and has a rib-vault over the passage with a lion in foliage on the central boss. Most of the outer portal of four orders decorated with chevrons is original, and also the spiral stair on the west side, but the two upper storeys and the single storey flanking wings containing porters' rooms were built for Bishop Barrington in the 1790s. The west side of the courtyard is filled by block 42m long which contains the great hall. Although 11th or 12th century work remains in the undercroft, and the main hall of the castle must have always been in this position, the existing hall above is in essence that built in the late 13th century by Bishop Bek. It has two original windows on the west side, although the buttresses and shallow porch facing the court are of the 1660s and the east windows are still more recent. Bishop Hatfield re-roofed the hall in the 1340s and built the south end as an extension it, but in the 1490s Bishop Fox divided this end off to create extra offices and thus returned the hall to its late 13th century dimensions of 30m by 10.5m. Also of the 1490s are the serving area west of the south end and the three huge fireplaces of the lofty kitchen to the SW, although there must have always been a kitchen hereabouts and the outer walls there are actually late 12th century, one original blocked window surviving in the SW fireplace. There is brickwork with decorative crenellation over two of the fireplaces. The kitchen and serving areas have retained their medieval purpose since the great hall now forms the university college dining hall. West of the great hall is a heavily buttressed 18th century terrace.

In a addition to a great hall for ceremonial purposes bishops usually had a smaller private hall for everyday use. At Durham this was provided in a north range, beyond which was a NE range containing the bishop's private rooms. The north range has a wedge-shaped NW tower and both it and the NE range may be late 11th century or early 12th century in their lowest parts, and it is possible that the original upper parts were of wood. Between the NE range and the motte is a Norman chapel thought to go back to the 1080s, with groined vaulting on six piers and round-headed east windows now obscured as a result of later enlargements of the motte encroaching upon it. The chapel seems to have been built against a still older wall (i.e. of the 1070s) containing a postern. The upper levels of the north range contain very fine late 12th century work remaining from Hugh de Puiset's private hall, although this room and his private chambers have been divided up and much altered. The doorway into his hall has three lavishly decorated and shafted orders with strings between them, the innermost order having rectangular sunk panels beaded diagonally, the middle one having rows of billets, and the outer one having sunk octagonal panels like coffering. The south wall of the Norman Gallery on the level above is arcaded internally with each window embrasure being flanked by smaller arches decorated with chevrons over seats with columns. The windows themselves are of 1752-3 and look out over the roof of the two storey gallery added in the 1530s. The seats prove that this level was always a habitable upper storey, not just an upper level of openings for the hall. In the southern re-entrant angle between the great hall and Tunstall's gallery is the Black Staircase, built by Bishop Cosin in 1662. The stair is typical of its period although the block containing it has windows built to match those of early 16th century staircase tower at the east end of the gallery. Two original but rather battered Norman two-light windows with semicircular heads open onto the upper part of the stair from the western end of the Norman Gallery.

The exterior of Tunstall's Chapel at Durham

The Norman chapel at Durham   *East hall doorway at Durham*

Bishop Tunstall's gallery connects with a projecting stair turret with a doorway at the bottom and the upper level has a doorway into the new chapel he built to supersede the very dark old Norman chapel, which was then closed off and forgotten for many years. In the south wall of the new chapel the three western windows are original work of the 1530s, whilst the other two windows are late 17th century work in the same style when the chapel was lengthened eastwards and its original east window was reset in the new east wall. The very fine stalls have come from the palace at Bishop Auckland and were made for Bishop Ruthall (1509-23).

The keep on the motte was entirely rebuilt in the 1840s to provide accommodation for university students, but old illustrations show that it is a fairly faithful reproduction of what Bishop Hatfield built in the 1340s to replace a 12th century structure. Crenellated walls 1.5m thick and 10m high enclose an irregular octagonal space 19m by 16m. At the corners buttresses are widened at the top to form turrets. The 14th century building had three storeys like the present structure, but there probably would have then been a tiny central court providing an internal light-well, as at Old Wardour in Wiltshire and Castle Rushen on the Isle of Man of about the same period. Excavations in 1951 found evidence that the motte had been heightened twice (probably c1130 and c1340). Towards the court the motte has a walled terrace at the summit and a 4m high buttressed retaining wall at the base. The rest of the circumference of the motte has two unwalled terraces, and a bottom terrace which is walled on the east and north, where it extends right along the north side of the castle. The topmost terrace probably goes back to the 14th century. The wall joining the keep to the gatehouse does not appear to contain any medieval work.

EDEN CASTLE   NZ 428388

Excavations east of the 18th century Castle Eden Hall in 1974 found a evidence of a ditch 11m wide and 1.4m deep with 12th and 13th century pottery and signs that the site was occupied until the 14th or 15th century. Shortly before Robert de Brus died in 1142 he granted his chapel here to the monks of Durham Cathedral, although he reserved the right for himself, his wife and his heir to have their own chaplain celebrate mass when they themselves were resident at Eden.

GATE CASTLE   NY 941379

A road to a cement works was built in the 1960s across the site of a tower house on the south side of the River Wear SW of Ludwell Farm. The very ruinous and featureless 2m thick walls of the lower part of a tower 17m long by 7m wide with a south wing 9m by 5m were demolished c1900 to provide materials for a new byre at the farm. There is a mention of a William Emerson of Gatecastle in 1619 and a mention of the tenement of Gatecastle in 1652.

HARTLEPOOL TOWN DEFENCES   NZ 527337   F

After a Scottish raid on Hartlepool in 1315 Edward II permitted the collecting of taxes for building a town wall. A wall about 600m long with about a dozen towers, some round and others square, closed off the western or landward side of a D-shaped promontory. The wall even extended across the harbour, which came further inland than now, except for a gate to admit ships. The section of wall that survives follows the shore on the south side and has in it a postern known as the Sandwell Gate with its portal flanked by triangular-fronted buttresses like breakwaters. The walls were said to be "fallen in many places" when the town was garrisoned by the rebel catholics during the revolt of 1569, but it is shown complete on a map of 1585. The Scots occupied the town in the 1640s and repaired the decayed walls. Traces of the western parts of the wall wall were examined by excavations in the 1980s.

Sandwell Gate at Hartlepool   *Window with sculpture at Holmside Hall*

The former gateway at Holmside

Hollinside Hall from the west

Hollinside Hall

HOLLINSIDE HALL   NZ 185599   F

A late 13th century hall block 16m by 7m over walls 0.9m thick is positioned so that the 4m square latrine turret at the NW corner overhangs a steep drop to the River Derwent. The upper storey has a two-light window at the west end wall and this end was perhaps divided off as a solar. The other end formed a service area and has a drain and a later window. On the south side the building has two wings, both apparently original although the east wall of the west wing is secondary to the entrance doorway between the wings. The SW wing has contained three levels of rooms, but none of them have any large windows or a fireplace. The SE wing contained a kitchen over a vaulted cellar. A new crosswall was later inserted to provide space for a staircase in front of the original main wall, and the re-entrant angle was then covered by a ribbed arch high up. Hollinside was occupied by the Harding family from the early 16th century until the early 18th century.

HOLMSIDE HALL   NZ 205497

Amongst the farm buildings are remains of a fortified manor house, probably with ranges around the north, east and south sides and a curtain wall on the west. The northern half (beyond a gateway arch demolished c1960) of the 1.4m thick curtain still rises 3.5m to the height of the wall-walk. The 7m wide and 38m long north range also survives in a much altered state, with a carved figure set in a blocked west window. Embedded in an outbuilding north of the farmhouse in the SW corner is the lower part of the south section of the curtain. A building about 14m by 7m with 15th to 16th century features occupying the eastern half of the southern side was taken down in 1966 after suffering from mining subsidence, and nothing remains of a possible east range. Extending 50m to the south is a ditched enclosure 65m wide, and old plans show that the area enclosed by ditches extended further NE. Holmside belonged to a family of that name before passing to the Umfravilles. It passed by marriage in the 15th century to Rowland Tempest. The estate was forfeited by Robert Tempest after the 1569 rebellion and it eventually passed to the Whittinghams.

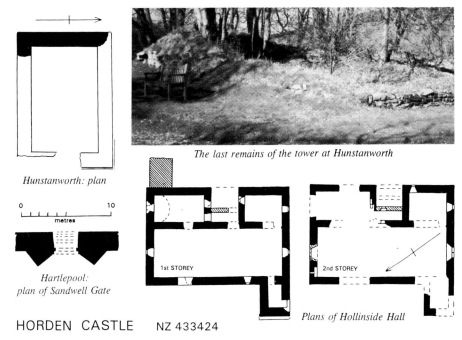

The last remains of the tower at Hunstanworth

Hunstanworth: plan

0   10

metres

Hartlepool:
plan of Sandwell Gate

1st STOREY

2nd STOREY

Plans of Hollinside Hall

HORDEN CASTLE   NZ 433424

The existing hall probably built by Sir John Conyers, with mullioned and transomed windows typical of the early 17th century, is thought to have replaced a three storey tower built here by Marmaduke Fitz-Geoffrey after he obtained a licence to crenellate in 1260. His son John was absent from home since he was governor of Perth and an inventory after his death in 1311 records only stock and farming equipment at Horden. After his heir was murdered at Durham in 1318 Horden passed to Thomas, Earl of Lancaster, who conveyed it to the Nolland family. It was purchased by John Menville in 1343 and later passed to William de Claxton. In 1411 the latter's widow was licensed to have a private chapel in her manor house at Horden. The house, described as of no value in 1431, passed to the Conyers family in 1484.

HOUGHTON-LE-SPRING RECTORY   NZ 340499

In 1483 Bishop Dudley fined and then pardoned John Kelyng for embattling his rectory here without a licence. It was later enlarged and was the residence until his death in 1583 of the celebrated divine Bernard Gilpin. The structure was mostly or entirely rebuilt in the late 17th century, only to be again replaced in the late 19th century. An old drawing suggests that the building was of three storeys and had a projection and a round corner turret facing a court with a gatehouse. See page 59.

HUNSTANWORTH TOWER   NY 949490   F

In the churchyard, immediately west of the church, lie the lower parts of a late medieval tower 10.5m wide by 14.4m long over walls 1.6m thick which presumably formed a secure residence for the vicar in this remote and exposed moorland location. Little remains of the east end except for the NE corner with a stepped plinth. The tumbled remains of the north wall seem to indicate that the basement was vaulted.

HYLTON CASTLE   NZ 358588   F

The de Hylton family may have had a house on this site by the end of the 11th century but on heraldic evidence the existing tower was built c1390-1406 by Sir William de Hylton. High up on the east side are carved Sir William's crest and the badge of Richard II. An inventory of 1448 describes it as a "gatehouse constructed of stone" and also mentions the chapel lying close by, and a hall, four chambers, a kitchen and two barns, which may have been of timber. In 1640 Henry Hilton bequeathed the castle to the Corporation of London and the Hiltons only recovered it after a long legal battle. In the early 18th century John Hilton added a north wing and remodelled the old tower, and the addition of a south wing by his son John made the building into a mansion nine bays long with a single storey bow-front pavilion in front of the old gateway inner portal on the east side. In 1746 the castle was left to Sir Richard Musgrave of Hayton in Cumbria with the provision that he change his name to Hilton. In the 1750s the castle was sold to the widow of Sir George Bowes but she never lived in it and by 1780 the building was in a neglected condition. It passed to the Earl of Strathmore and then in 1812 was acquired by Simon Temple. His attempt to restore the building was thwarted when he ran out of funds. Eventually, in 1862 the building was purchased by William Briggs. He demolished the wings and modernised the main tower was modernised, the 18th century pedimented windows shown on old prints being replaced by windows more gothic in character. The castle was later purchased by the Wearmouth Coal Company but it remained unoccupied and in the 1950s the ruinous shell (threatened with demolition) was taken into State guardianship.

Hylton Castle

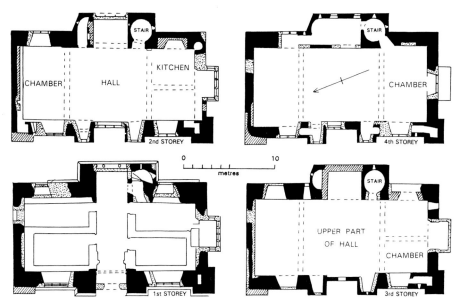

Plans of Hylton Castle

The tower measures 21.4m by 10.9m over walls 1.6m thick above the plinth. The centre of each long side projects out, and there are machicolated parapets on the east, west and south sides, but not at the north end, where a barn or stable or something similar must have adjoined from the start. The west projection is recessed between square turrets flanking the outer portal which was closed by a portcullis and has high above it a spectacular display of carved heraldic shields. The outer corners also have square turrets, and all four turrets are corbelled out as octagons at the top with machicolations. However, the present symmetry of the turrets dates only from the 1860s, and the medieval layout was rather different. The NW corner did not project, and until c1730 it had a circular bartizan matching that surviving on the NE corner. There is another circular bartizan, although smaller, upon the SE corner.

The medieval layout had two cellars north of the gateway passage and two rooms for guards or porters on the south, with a latrine in the south wall and a well. The passage and all four rooms were vaulted before they were internally reduced in thickness. The 1860s layout has a single reception room on either side of the passage, that on the south having a large bay window. Off the passage (still blocked except for a modest west doorway) leads a spiral stair in the east projection leading to the upper rooms and the battlements. The second storey contained an almost square central hall with windows piercing the central turrets. A private chamber with a latrine in the NW corner lay north of it, and a kitchen and another service room to the south. Until subdivided in the 16th century the hall was it was open to the roof. There was another chamber over that on the north (reached by a second staircase from the hall), whilst on the south there was a small chamber over the service room and then a larger room over both it and the lofty kitchen. These rooms must have had fireplaces in the lost crosswalls and only the kitchen now retains a fireplace, together with an oven. Between the two staircases there was space for two tiny chapels, one above the other, and three levels of bedrooms, two of which retain their original windows, the uppermost bedroom being at the level of the main battlements.

Old print of Hylton Castle in 1844

The ruined chapel of St Catherine at Hylton is also early 15th century, although much altered and incorporating a reset keeled shaft of the 13th century in a south buttress. The arch at the west end and the evidence of the Bucks' print suggests the building originally had a short nave extending to the west. Polygonal-ended transepts were added on either side of the surviving chancel in the mid to late 16th century. In the later medieval period there were several chantries to members of the family.

KIRK MERRINGTON NZ 262315 F

In 1144 William Comyn built a rampart around this hill-top cruciform Norman church with a central tower, but it was soon captured by supporters of the lawful bishop, William de St Barbara. The present church on the site dates only from 1850.

LAMBTON CASTLE NZ 299527

Lambton House is a much altered 17th century brewhouse beside the site of the original seat of the Lambton family (referred to as "of Lambton Castle"), demolished in 1797, although it is uncertain whether any medieval work survived within it. By then the family had transferred to Harraton Hall on the opposite bank of the Wear, which William Henry Lambton had recently inherited. This building was then extended and renamed Lambton Castle.

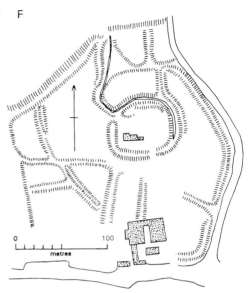

Low Dinsdale: site plan

Langley Hall

Langley Hall

LANGLEY HALL   NZ 211466   V

On a spur above a tributary of the River Browney are overgrown ruins of two 9m wide ranges set about 24m apart of a 16th century moated house built by Henry, Lord Scrope. Of the west range there remain 20m of the 1.2m thick east wall and also the thicker north end wall with openings for three low unvaulted storeys. The east range was of just two storeys and has latrine shutes in a projection halfway along what remains of the east side, south of which are two doorways in the outer wall. The hall may have been in the north range with the gateway in the south range.

LOW BUTTERBY MANOR   NZ 276394

The stone-lined moat surrounding the 17th and 18th century farmhouse with later alterations now only remains on the NE. Surviving until fairly recently was a gatehouse with a round-arched portal with mullioned windows above, those of the third storey being in a gable of the roof. A sundial upon it was dated 1706.

LOW DINSDALE MANOR   NZ 346110

The manor house seems to be a 19th century casing of an older building, possibly medieval, and the home of the Surtees family since the 12th century. The house lies within a moated platform 55m by 45m. It and another platform to the north are surrounded by other spacious earthwork enclosures. Foundations of a stone gatehouse are said to have been found here. See plan on page 39.

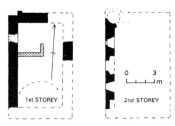

Plans of Ludworth Tower

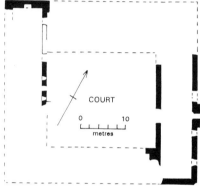

Plan of Langley Hall

Ludworth Tower

LUDWORTH TOWER   NZ 357413   F

West of the village are remains of a tower 11.6m long by 7.5m wide which Bishop Thomas Langley licensed Thomas Holden to crenellate in 1422. The manor had previously belonged to the de Ludworths, and was purchased in 1438 by the Newcastle merchant Roger de Thornton, although his father may have had possession earlier. In 1483 the manor passed by marriage to the Lumleys and in 1566 it went to Sir Richard Bellasis. The building is thought to have been ruinous by 1680, when the property was sold to Sir Ralph Carr. Most of the east and south sides collapsed in 1890 but the west wall still stands 12m high with part of the basement vault with a room divided off in the NW corner. The second storey had west windows set on either side of a fireplace and a latrine at the SW corner. The third storey had a similar layout, but with only one west-facing window, and there was a fourth storey, also with a fireplace. A 19th century description suggests that the entrance lay in the north wall by the spiral stair in the projecting NW corner linking the upper rooms, and that there was a barmkin to the east where there are buried foundations. However it is more likely that the tower formed the solar block of a hall east of it with service rooms beyond it. A late 18th century sketch of the building shows a single storey range adjoining the tower north wall, on which was the gable mark of a higher and wider older range. There was also a projection from the west end of the south wall. The parapet survived on the north end wall and at the SW corner, and the NW stair turret rose slightly above it.

LUMLEY CASTLE   NZ 289511   H

Sir Ralph Lumley obtained a licence to crenellate from the Bishop of Durham in 1389, and an additional licence in 1392 from Richard II. The building then constructed survives complete although partly refaced and remodelled. Lying above the east bank of the River Wear, it comprises four ranges set around a court 30m by 22m, the west range containing the 30m long hall being about 13m wide, whilst the others are from 8 to 9m wide and contain three storeys. At the corners are rectangular four storey towers, those at the NE and SE corners having diagonal buttresses surmounted by turrets on their single outermost corners and being 10.7m wide with lengths of 14.3m and 15.2m respectively. The western towers have diagonal buttresses on both their western corners and are 11m wide by 19m long. These towers are less massive than the others and may represent a different campaign of work i.e. c1405 as opposed to c1390, perhaps after the original house built c1300 by Sir Robert Lumley, and altered c1350 by Sir Marmaduke Lumley, had been swept away. Sir Ralph died during a short lived rebellion against Richard II and the castle probably remained incomplete for about a decade until Henry IV restored the estate to his son John in 1404. There are several other anomalies as regards wall thicknesses in the castle. The south range, for instance, has a thick wall towards the court and a thinner one towards the field (perhaps because of rebuilding), the opposite of what one might expect. The NW tower has triple service doorways at the north end of the hall and contained a lofty kitchen, whilst the NE tower contains a chapel, rib-vaulted in two bays. The gateway lies in the middle of the east side and is flanked by square turrets and is surmounted by shields with the arms of Richard II and the Lumleys, Percies, Nevilles, Greys and Hyltons. Higher up is a richly cusped arch between the turrets, behind which are machicolations. There are two polygonal turrets set in the middle of the west wall of the courtyard but the entrance beneath them leads only into a vaulted cellar. The hall above was reached only by one of the spiral stairs located in the four corners of the court. The set of eighteen armorial shields between the polygonal turrets and the lavabos set onto the base of each one date from c1580, when John, Lord Lumley made extensive alterations to the building, including the many mullioned and transomed windows in the walls facing the courtyard.

NE tower at Lumley Castle

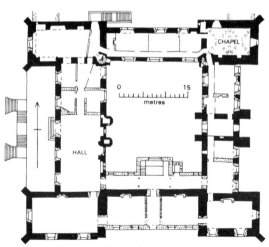

Plan of Lumley Castle

Old print of Lumley Castle

Old print of the NW corner of the courtyard at Lumley Castle

During the Civil War the castle was occupied by Sir William Langley, brother-in-law of the then owner Sir Richard Lumley who was away down south serving King Charles. A later Sir Richard Lumley was created Earl of Scarborough in 1690 and he and his son again remodelled the castle, the son, at least employing Sir John Vanbrugh as his architect. A service court was added on the north side, sash windows were inserted throughout the exterior facades, the state rooms in the south range and the SW and SE towers were refurbished, and a corridor was added on the south side of the court with a projection in the middle to contain a scale-and-platt staircase. In the north and east ranges corridors have been provided by internal divisions. The northern part of the hall was divided up whilst the rest became the entrance hall of the reorientated building, the original gateway of which faces the steep drop to the river rather than towards the easy approach. The west entrance then created is modest but there is a cupola at the top. The hall retains two original medieval windows on the east side, whilst a fireplace of c1580 with the Lumley arms on the overmantel is set into where there was once a third. Other medieval windows survive in the saloon in the SE tower and in the chapel east wall in the NE tower.

Heraldry above the gateway at Lumley

By the early 19th century the Earls of Scarborough had abandoned the castle as a residence, although it was not allowed to fall into ruin and saw some use by the family in the early 20th century. In the 1950s and 60s the castle was leased to Durham University. It is now a luxury hotel and restaurant.

SW tower at Lumley Castle

West end of solar block at Muggleswick Grange

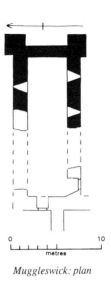

Muggleswick: plan

Muggleswick Grange

MIDDLETON ST GEORGE CASTLE   NZ 345122

The 19th century Tower Hill House takes its name from a motte rising 6m to a summit 20m across in its grounds on the north bank of the Tees. The castle guarded a ford and was probably built by the Bairds, who held the manor until 1367.

MUGGLESWICK GRANGE   NZ 046501   V

Muggleswick belonged to the monks of Durham and a grange was built in 1260s by Prior Hugh, although the existing building 17m long by 7.5m wide over walls 1.5m thick may be slightly later. It has a blocked three-light window high up with a fireplace below it. The end wall containing these features is flanked by square corner turrets with corbelled parapets but the wall itself was gabled without a parapet. The farm building to the SW represents the last remains of the undercroft of a hall.

OLD DURHAM CASTLE   NZ 287420

Until destroyed in the first half of the 19th century a motte and bailey surrounded by a ditch 10m wide lay on the east bank of the River Wear 1.2km east of the cathedral.

POCKERLEY MANOR   NZ 223545   O

Most of the buildings on the Beamish Museum site have been imported from elsewhere but this stronghouse lies in its original position. Dendro-dating techniques have recently shown that the roof is mid 15th century. The house contained a hall and chamber end to end over a vaulted basement, with sleeping lofts in the roof, the stairs being in an end wall. The two-light window on the north is original but the three-light window on the south is a convincing-looking fake of 1999.

RABY CASTLE   NZ 129218   O

In 1131 Algar, Prior of Durham, granted Raby to Dolfin, who was married to a niece of Bishop Flambard. Their grandson Robert Fitz-Maldred married the heiress Isobel de Neville and thus also obtained Brancepeth and Sheriff Hutton. Their son Geoffrey took his mother's surname. The oldest parts of the castle at Raby were built either by Ranulph, 1st Lord Neville, or (more likely) his son Ralph, who succeeded him in 1331. Ralph was captured by the Douglases in a fight at Berwick in 1319 in which his elder brother Robert was killed, but in 1346 his fortune was made when he in turn defeated and captured King David II of Scotland at Neville's Cross. Raby seems to have been a stronghouse rather than a castle before additions were made in the 1370s by his son John, who obtained a licence to crenellate from Richard II in 1378, probably to ratify work then nearing completion. His son Ralph, who succeeded in 1389, was created Earl of Westmorland by Richard II in 1397 and he was given additional honours for his help in placing Henry IV on the throne in 1399. By then the family had also built palatial castles at Brancepeth and Sheriff Hutton and they had a fourth with Earl Ralph's later rebuilding of the castle at Middleham. The youngest daughter of Earl Ralph and his second wife Lady Joan Beaufort was Cecily, who married Richard, Duke of York and thus became mother of Edward IV and Richard III.

The inner gatehouse at Raby Castle

The outer gatehouse at Raby Castle

The 2nd and 3rd Earls were succeeded by their grandsons in 1484 and 1523 respectively. Henry, who became 5th Earl in 1549, took part as a boy in the Pilgrimage of Grace of 1536. He and his son Charles, 6th Earl, remained Catholic after the Reformation and the latter was forfeited by Elizabeth I for his part in the rebellion of 1569, after which he escaped into a long exile in Holland. The castle was retained by the Crown until sold in 1626 to Sir Henry Vane (who had leased it since 1616), whose main seat was Fairlawn in Kent. He served on Charles I's Privy Council and was made Secretary of State in 1640, but lost the post after the attainder and execution of Thomas Strafford, and supported the Parliamentary cause during the Civil War. His son Sir Henry the Younger was later imprisoned by Cromwell on the Isle of Wight in 1656 and in 1662 was executed by Charles II. His son Christopher was a Privy Councillor under James II but later supported William III and in 1698 was created Baron Barnard. The baron attempted to dismantle the castle in order to disinherit his son Gilbert because he disapproved of his choice of wife but a court order was made forcing the baron to desist and to rebuild the damaged parts. Further work on the castle continued after Gilbert finally inherited it in 1723. His son Henry was created Earl of Darlington by George II in 1754. The third earl, William was made Duke of Cleveland by William IV in 1833. His three sons all became duke in turn but left no children, so in 1891 the dukedom became extinct whilst Henry de Vere, a descendant of a younger son of Gilbert, 2nd Lord Barnard, inherited that title as 9th Lord Barnard, along with Raby. The castle is still owned by the 11th Lord Barnard.

The Bulmer Tower at Raby Castle

The original building of the early or mid 14th century had a central court 22m square with a hall range 12m wide on the east side, a west range 11m wide which contained a gateway with a portcullis groove, and a south range 9m wide. On the north lies an L-shaped tower known as the Keep which is less altered and perhaps slightly earlier than the rest of the building. It has a main block about 11m by 9.5m, west of which there was a short length of curtain walling containing a postern. Clustered round the outside of the building are several other towers, generally slightly larger than the Keep, which forms one of a group of three clustered around the service area north of the hall, the others being the Kitchen Tower on the north, and Mount Raskelf to the east. The Kitchen Tower has squinch arches to support a lantern roof, and a wall passage through the upper windows. The Keep and Mount Raskelf both have rib-vaulted basements. South of Mount Raskelf is the Chapel Tower, with a back entrance below the chapel itself, which has an east window of 1901. At the original NW corner is the Watch Tower, and at the SW corner is Joan's Tower, both of which gave flanking protection to the gateway. Later alterations have removed another tower which contained the principal apartments south of the hall and a possible second tower SE of the hall, although the later Bulmer Tower beyond where it would have been is said to have been detached during the medieval period.

The south side of Raby Castle

The original building was considerably altered in the 1370s. A new upper hall was built over the old one, which thus became a lower hall for the use of servants. The upper hall retains paired lancets with transoms of c1370. Joan's Tower at the SW corner was more than doubled in size to produce a structure 22m long by 13m wide with a wedge-shaped turret projecting from the NW corner. The original part of the building was given an extra storey in the 1770s. A small triangular second court was created on the north side by adding a range with a (later rebuilt) machicolated parapet and a curtain wall (also machicolated and containing a postern) at right angles to each other and capping the angle with the boldly projecting Clifford's Tower which measures 20.5m by 12.5m and rises through five storeys to a height of 24m. This tower retains three 14th century windows, the others being of c1870. An outer part with a lierne-vaulted passage and a second portcullis in the outer portal was added in front of the gateway to create what is known as the Neville Gateway. On the outer corners are square turrets which project diagonally, but not at 45 degrees towards the angle since they incline more towards the portal, above which are the arms of the Nevilles, St George and the Latimers, and then machicolations. Extra apartments were provided within the pentagonal Bulmer's Tower 11.5m wide added beyond the original private apartments south of the hall. This tower differs from the others in being built of millstone grit. As in Clifford's Tower the vaults of the upper levels were removed in a remodelling of the 1840s to provide extra bedrooms.

Also of the 1370s is the surrounding irregularly oval outer court 115m by 100m with a curtain wall originally 10m high externally (but now much cut down to just a parapet internally) surrounded by a moat fed from a lake on the south side and flanked by numerous small rectangular turrets. On the north is an outer gatehouse 9m by 7.5m of somewhat irregular plan with machicolated turrets and stone figures at the summit. The short sections of walling ending in turrets on either side of the gatehouse are 18th century.

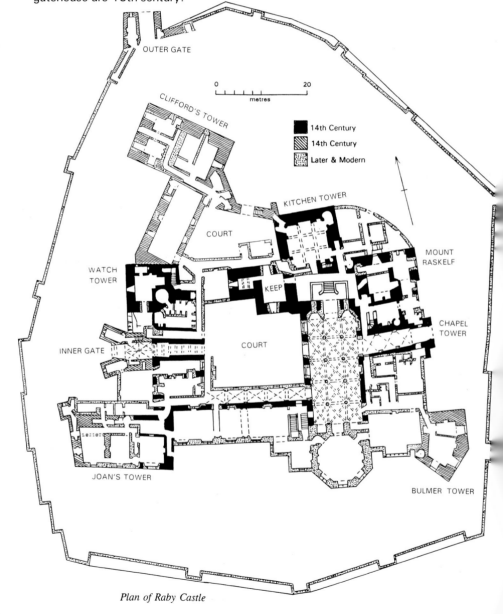

Plan of Raby Castle

Machicolations over inner gate at Raby

The courtyard and keep at Raby Castle

The principal private apartments of the original early to mid 14th century layout at Raby were remodelled in the mid 17th century, and again in mid 18th century, whilst an extra storey was added in the 1770s, when a connecting corridor was inserted alongside them in the courtyard. A 19th century octagon has replaced a round tower of the 1770s which itself replaced the original solar tower, which was gutted by a fire c1725. The upper hall now extends into the octagon to make a room 39m long by 11m wide. Its roof has been replaced and its east windows blocked by the addition of a range in the re-entrant angle between the hall and the projecting towers at either end. Because the inner court was too small to turn a coach a through system was made possible in the 1770s by knocking a doorway into the vaulted lower hall, allowing coaches to disembark in this hall and then leave through the back gateway. In order to obtain enough height for what thus became an entrance hall with a new quadripartite vault, the Lower Hall floor was lowered and the Upper Hall floor was raised. Also of that period were the offices hidden behind a wall curving round across the re-entrant angle between the Kitchen Tower and Mount Raskelf, and the passage leading west from the kitchen to the old vaulted guard room south of Clifford's Tower, which then became a servants' hall. The rooms above the latter were then remodelled to form the Hunters' Gallery.

The Old Lodge

The Old Lodge in Raby Park

RABY OLD LODGE   NZ 090222

Plans of the Old Lodge

On a shelf above the north side of the Langley Beck 4km west of the castle is a three storey late 15th or early 16th century tower known as the Old Lodge which served as the park keeper's residence. An embattled building with a box-machicolation over the entrance on the south side, it measures 11.9m by 7.7m over walls ranging from 1m to 1.7m in thickness. The vulnerable north side is flanked by a wing 4.5m projecting 2.3m from its western end. The wing contains a staircase which could only be reached from the entrance by crossing the basement room, which was a kitchen with a fireplace with an oven in the east end wall. In more recent times a new entrance with a single storey porch has been built adjacent to the wing. The second storey has a 2.5m wide recess at the west end and it appears that there was once a fine oriel window here. At this level the windows at each end of the south wall are original, but the other openings are later insertions.

RAVENSWORTH CASTLE   NZ 233591

Lying derelict in the stableyard are two of the four rectangular corner towers of the castle of the Lumley family. The towers are 9m high, of three storeys, and lay at the SE and NE corners of a rectangular court which is said to have had a ditch 12m wide. The NE tower measures 7.3m by 6m and the SE tower measures 8.5m by 6.3m. The unusual recessing of the upper walls between clasping pilaster buttresses rising flush from the lower walls up to projecting parapet (now mostly missing) is original since the towers are shown in this manner on a Buck brothers engraving of 1728. The engraving suggests that a third tower then survived in the NW corner (and perhaps the fourth in a cut-down state as an adjunct of the new house), and that the south curtain wall was then still intact. A 2m long section of this wall, which was about 4m high to the wall-walk, still adjoins the SE tower and both towers have similar lengths of the former east curtain adjoining them. The cross-loops in these short sections of walling appear to be original. Both towers contain original lancet windows and straight staircases. They have vaulted basements, and the NE tower contains a vaulted second storey room with a fireplace in the north wall. The castle probably had a hall range on the west side and perhaps a central gatehouse on the east. There is no evidence that it had ranges of apartments integrated with the curtain walls so it was probably an early 14th century building more like Etal or Ford in Northumberland than the later 14th century castles at Lumley, Bolton, Sheriff Hutton or Wressle.

The castle passed by marriage to Marmaduke Lumley in 1385 and remained with his descendants until it passed to Henry Boynton in 1497. It passed in the 1530s to Sir Henry Gascoyne, and in 1607 was sold by Sir William Gascoyne to the Newcastle merchant Thomas Liddell. His son Thomas was made a baronet by Charles I for his defence of Newcastle against the Scots in 1642. One of the Lidells built a new house on the west side of the court in 1724 and this was "altered and improved" (involving breaching the curtain wall with an extension) in the 1750s for Henry Liddell, who had been created Lord Ravenworth in 1747. Another new house replacing it was erected for Sir Thomas Liddell, for whom the title Lord Ravensworth was resurrected in 1821. This eventually became a substantial embattled structure and remained the Liddells residence until it became a school in the 1920s. Demolition threatened in the 1930s was postponed because of the outbreak of war, but finally carried out in 1953.

The SE tower at Ravensworth

REDMARSHALL RECTORY NZ 387212

Bishop Lawrence Booth granted Rector Adam Morland a licence to crenellate his rectory at Redmarshall in 1462. The licence was issued in conjunction with a pardon since Morland had already embattled the rectory without permission. The tower is thought to have stood on the site of the present rectory until c1833. An illustration of 1788 shows a three storey tower with a corbelled parapet which had been given rectangular sash windows matching those of an added three storey wing.

RYTON CASTLE NZ 151648 V

The church lies high above the River Tyne and occupies a bailey platform 75m by 60m of a motte on the north rising 3.5m above its ditch to a summit 9m across.

SADBERGE CASTLE NZ 341167 F

The small church of 1831 and its graveyard occupy the summit of a mound up to 5m high originally commanding an extensive view. The mound measures 37m across on top and is divided from a possible bailey site to the east by a 15m wide ditch 3m deep said to have once contained water. A ditch on the north side was filled in in 1806. The castle was probably built by Bishop Hugh de Puiset after he purchased the manor from Richard I in 1189. Hutchinson claimed to have seen a document referring to the manor of Aslakby being held in return for castle-guard at Sadberge.

SOCKBURN CASTLE NZ 350070

A raised area about 60m square to the south of the hall of the 1830s, close to the ruined Saxon church, is the only relic of a manor house which Sir Christopher Conyers was licensed by Bishop Lawrence Booth to crenellate in 1470. The family held Sockburn from the 11th century until in 1653 it passed by marriage to Francis Talbot, who inherited the earldom of Shrewsbury the following year. The castle later passed to the Stoners family and was sold to Sir Edward Blackett, but it had been demolished by the end of the 18th century.

The Stone House (former rectory) at Stanhope

STANHOPE CASTLE   NY 996392

Suthbert Rippon's house of 1798 with extensions of 1875 lies on the site of a castle mentioned in a deed issed by Bishop Anthony Bek c1300. Two 18th century descriptions suggest it had an oblong court about 25m wide enclosed by an ashlar faced wall and protected on the naturally weak east and north sides by a deep ditch. The Stone House above the north side of the churchyard (at 997394) is an early 17th century bastle-type building of three storeys which formed the rectory until a new one was built in 1697. One doorway and the top storey windows are original.

STOCKTON CASTLE   NZ 446186

The Castle shopping centre and car park at the south end of the High Street lie on the site of a castle of the bishops of Durham of which an "embattled cowhouse" (actually part of a tower) survived in use as a barn until the 1860s. The building lay within a wedge-shaped platform 180m by 150m with the River Tees on the east and a moat up to 50m wide on the other sides. Part of this moat, by then dry, survived into the 20th century. A drawing of 1647 depicts a quadrangular court with round corner towers and square intermediate towers, i.e. a southern English type of plan typified by Bodiam Castle in Sussex, not at all the type normally found in northern England. Bishop Kellaw is said to have fortified this site in 1311-16 but the stonework may have been later, and the first mention of a castle here is in 1376, when a ward of Bishop Thomas Hatfield was abducted from it. In 1543 Henry VIII had the castle repaired at a cost of £36 and a garrison installed. Further maintenance, including the provision of new gates, was undertaken in 1554. A survey commissioned by Bishop Richard Barnes in 1577 refers to a hall 19m long by 10m wide as being "roofless and ruinous". Two 11m high towers on the north side were in need of repointing. That "north of the chapel" was a substantial building 14m long by 12m wide. The survey also mentions a large kitchen, a horse driven mill, a kiln, brewhouse, bakehouse, a buttery and wine cellar, a stable, a "tower over the stairs" (probably a porch) and two walled gardens. The castle was damaged by fire in 1597 and was captured by the Scottish army in 1644 from a Royalist garrison. After the Scottish army withdrew in 1647 extra outer fortifications recently erected by it were dismantled by order of Parliament before the castle was sold to William Underwood and James Nelthorpe. Much of the building had been dismantled by 1652, although it still had a bailiff and keeper six years later.

STREATLAM CASTLE   NZ 083199

This castle was called "Newcastle" originally and seems to have been built after the estate passed by marriage from the de la Hay family to John de Trayne. It passed by marriage to Adam de Bowes in 1310 in was rebuilt by Sir William Bowes in the mid 15th century. Leland in the 1530s described the castle as having "two or three towers and a fair stable". During the 1569 rebellion the castle was captured by the rebels after a seven day siege. Sir George Bowes, who held out at Barnard Castle, described his seat at Streatlam as being wrecked by the rebels, who removed all the glass and iron bars of the windows, the ceilings and doors and the lead roofs. It was must have been repaired since Sir George died within it in 1580. Sir William Bowes, who died in 1706, remodelled the castle but a later visitor wrote that as a result the house was not very comfortable or conveniently laid out, the site being rather narrow and confined. In the 1770s the castle passed to the earls of Strathmore. It remained in use until partly demolished in the 1920s, the last traces of the ditch having vanished half a century earlier. The last remaining parts were blown up in 1959.

SUMMERHOUSE   NZ 202190

There indications here of a moated platform 35m by 30m with a former curtain wall and the base of a tower, and of a second, larger moated enclosure.

THORNLEY CASTLE   NZ 360383

Thornley Hall has a naturally strong defensive site and may have been the location of the castle built by Bishop William de St Barbe in 1143 against the usurper William Comyn. In 1144 it was handed over by Hugh Pinton to Comyn's nephew, who in turn allowed it to be occupied by Henry, Earl of Northumberland, son of King David of Scotland. The garrisoned terrorised the neighbourhood until the earl withdrew to Scotland later in the year, after which the site was probably abandoned.

WALWORTH CASTLE   NZ 231189   H

Walworth was long held by the Hansards as tenants of the bishops of Durham. It passed by marriage to the Ayscough family and in 1579 they sold the hall (the castle appellation is recent) to Thomas Jenison, Auditor General of Ireland. He remodelled what Hutchinson described in 1794 as a "heap of ruins" into an Elizabethan mansion. His widow entertained James VI of Scotland here in 1603 on his way south to claim the English throne. The building was altered in the 1740s by Ralph Jennison and again in the 1850s after being sold to the Aylmer family, most of the mullion-and-transom windows being of that period. By the 1930s the building was occupied only tenants and in 1950 it was purchased by Durham County Council for use as a special school. It was then reroofed and a number of 18th century interior details were lost during alterations. Since being sold off in 1980 the building has been used as a hotel.

Walworth Castle

The castle consists of four ranges around a small court which has now been roofed over. Parts of the building are of two storeys but the south and west ranges have three storeys and at the SW and SE corners are round towers about 6m in diameter. The south wing has walls 1m thick and is probably medieval. Towards the west end the south wall has a slight change in alignment all the way up which may mark the dividing wall between a hall to the east, and a solar to the west. The west wing adjoins it at an oblique angle and is also probably medieval, although its west wall was rebuilt in 1851. The SW tower probably dates from the 1530s or 1540s since it has walls 1.3m thick and blocked dumb-bell shaped loops flanking the adjacent wings. The small blocked loops, one round-headed and another trefoil-headed look like medieval features reset, perhaps from an ecclesiastical building demolished around the Reformation period. Round corner towers of this type appear in mid to late 16th century castellated houses in Scotland but Dawdon (see p25) is the only other tower or mansion in the North of England with surviving remains of such a feature. The dumb-bell shaped loops again have parallels in Scotland and in Henry VIII's forts of the 1540s on the south coast of England but no other examples survive in northern England. The tower was remodelled in the late 16th century to match the SE tower then added, and was given new south-facing windows on each level in the 1850s. The wing of the 1950s projecting west from the west range north end replaced a older stable block, possibly late 16th century.

WESTGATE CASTLE   NY 907382

This castle stood in High Westgate between the Middlehope Burn and road to Allenheads. Plaster and lime (but no masonry) was found on the site in the 1980s. The castle seems to have served as a hunting lodge by the west entrance to Stanhope Park but in the 15th century it was used as a prison. In 1442 it was granted for life to Thomas, Lord Lumley, the bishop's "Master Forester in Weardale", but it was repaired at the bishop's expense in the 1470s whilst Lord Thomas was still alive. In 1493 Bishop John Shirwood ordered the tower to be made into "a habitable house of nine rooms". Leland described it as a "pretty square pile on the north side of the Were River, and refers to the leaded roof, fair hall, great chamber, buttery and pantry. In the 1560s Bishop Pilkington partly demolished the tower but he was ordered to make the tower defensible again and re-roof it with slates. A report of 1590 suggests the tower was about 18m long by 9m wide and had a small gatehouse adjoining it. Repairs so that the tower could be used for holding Forest courts were ordered in 1596. The castle may have been wrecked during the Civil War and only ruined walls remained in 1647. It remained thus until mostly dismantled for materials to build an adjacent school c1800. Buried vaults and foundations survived until the early 20th century and may still partly exist under modern boundary walls.

Houghton-le-Spring Rectory

Gunloop at Walworth

Witton Tower

WITTON CASTLE   NZ 154305   H

The tower house and barmkin above the south side of the River Wear are assumed to date from 1410, when Sir Ralph Eure was pardoned by Bishop Thomas Langley for building an unlicensed castle and was granted a licence for its crenellation. The next Eure, another Ralph, was slain at Townton in 1461, and William Eure was made Warden of the East March in the 1530s and a baron in 1544. William, 4th Lord Eure sold the castle c1622 to Sir Richard Forster and in 1637 it was sold again, this time to William Darcy. He garrisoned the castle for the king in the 1640s but it was eventually captured by Sir Arthur Hazlerigg. The building was then stripped of its fittings but the walls survived intact until there was a dismantling of some of the barmkin buildings by James Darcy, created Lord Darcy of Navan in 1721. His grandson James Jessop succeeded him as the 2nd Lord Darcy and in 1743 sold the ruin to William Cuthbert for £15000. It passed by marriage to the Hopper family, who created a new house west of the old tower. This was damaged by fire in 1797, and not fully restored until after it was purchased in 1816 by William Chaytor. It was sold to Donald Maclean in 1839 but he went bankrupt and the castle was recovered by the Chaytors. Now part of the Lambton estate, it is used as a leisure centre.

The tower house at Witton Castle

Witton Castle from the NE

The barmkin has a wall 1.5m thick rising 6m to a wall-walk and parapet and enclosing a court 47m by 52. The box machicolations over the gateways in the east and west walls may not be medieval, and it is possible that the existing parapet on the barmkin is a replacement of the 1760s or 70s of the original one since the very boldly corbelled-out bartizan on the SE corner looks more like an 18th century sentry-box than medieval work. However, there is a more convincing round bartizan on the NE corner and the chamber with latrine shoots overhanging the SW corner looks old. The gateways lack drawbar slots and there are signs of a possible older gateway further south on the east side. The thinly walled three storey clock tower projecting entirely internally on the south side is a 16th century addition. A third gateway just west of it and a fourth just west of the NE corner are probably 17th century.

Old print of Witton Castle

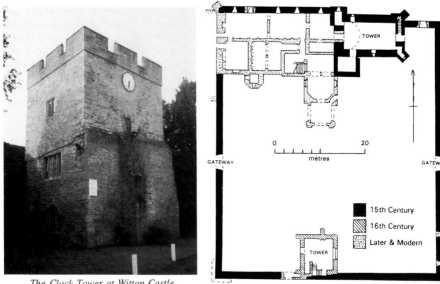

The Clock Tower at Witton Castle

Plan of Witton Castle

A 19th century castellated house has replaced the hall block which occupied the western half of the north side, although the thick outer wall there looks at least partly medieval. The tower house east of it stands complete but with 19th century windows for the two upper storeys lying over a vaulted basement still lighted only by two narrow loops. The tower measures 15.7m by 9m over walls 1.6m thick and has diagonal buttresses at the east corners with the sides corbelled out at the top as machicolated turrets. A spiral stair in a 4m square NW turret connects the upper levels and a service stair leads down to an inserted basement doorway in the east wall. A larger turret 6m wide projecting 4.2m from the west end of the south wall must be slightly later since it is not bonded with the main building. It has carved figures on the parapet. The second storey has a fireplace with an externally projecting breast between the two south windows. Old drawings show the east wall of a chapel with remains of a traceried window adjoining the SE corner of this turret.

Witton Castle from the SE

WITTON TOWER   NZ 143313   V

Formerly known as Witton Hall, this building lies at the west end of the main street of Witton-le-Wear. The three storey block about 13m by 6.5m in the middle has been described as a much-altered medieval tower house but it only has walls 0.7m thick and there is no certain evidence that it predates its oldest features, which are the 17th century rusticated quoins at the southern corners and the staircase filling the northern third of the building. The south windows are 19th century but older mullion- and transom windows appear on the west side. The east wing appears to be entirely 19th century but the two storey west wing may contain medieval work. It shows signs of a number of blocked older features, although it is thinly walled and has no windows earlier than the 18th century. The chapel block beyond looks medieval at a glance but in fact only the lowest part of it contains pre-17th century walling.

OTHER POSSIBLE FORTIFIED BUILDINGS IN COUNTY DURHAM

CASTLE STEADS NZ 179428 Former stone building within a moated platform.
OLD HALL FARM, High Coniscliffe, has wing with vault, upper lancet, latrine shutes.
BELLASIS, EVENWOOD, SNOTTERTON and WHESSOE GRANGE had moated houses.
WARDLEY HALL lies in a moated enclosure 190m by 120m. Possible mottes lie at:
BLACKWELL NZ 274130, EGGLESCLIFFE NZ 426132, & IRESHOPEBURN NY 871385

BASTLE HOUSES

Bastle houses were built by tenant farmers and those of similar rank in response to the threat of raids and general lawlessness which became endemic in the border counties during the 1580s and lasted until the border was pacified c1610. Wealth was then measured in cattle, which were liable to be stolen by any neighbouring clan who were short of food. Most bastles had a single living room set over a byre for livestock which had its own separate entrance. The byres were sometimes vaulted, but the majority had huge beams to carry the upper floor. A hatch allowed the person that secured the byre door to reach the upper room. The upper room had small windows with iron stanchions, a doorway reached by a ladder (often later replaced in stone) and a fireplace at the far end. Bastles were intended only for passive resistance to raids never lasting longer than the hours of darkness. They are not equipped with machicolations, wall-walks with embattled parapets, turrets, or loops designed for discharging bows or firearms, nor do they normally contain latrines or staircases. Over 200 bastles are known in Northumberland (see the Northumberland volume in this series for a more detailed discussion of their design and purpose) and in recent years a small number of such buildings has been recognised in Weardale.

BONNYMOOR & HARTHOPBURN NY 883378 Made out of one thick-walled house.
BRIDGE END NY 852407 Gable-headed basement doorway. Rebuilt upper storey.
KILLHOPEBURN SHIELING NY 835417 Oldest part of ruin is 6.3m square over walls
   0.9m thick with blocked round-headed doorway. Many lockers in upper storey.
SWINHOPEBURN NY 909375 Nearly square three storey building forms core of
   western farmhouse. Blocked original doorway in east wall. Upper parts rebuilt.
WEST BLACKDENE & AMRITA COTTAGE NY 867391 Altered thick-walled houses.
Described in the main gazetteer are bastles of a superior three storey type at Baal Hill
   House, near Wolsingham; Pockerley, an original in-situ building in the Beamish
   Museum; and Stone House, a former rectory in the village of Stanhope. Pockerley
   and Baal Hill House appear to predate the main bastle period of c1590-1620.

GLOSSARY OF TERMS

ASHLAR - Masonry of blocks with even faces and square edges. BAILEY - defensible space enclosed by a wall or a palisade and ditch. BARBICAN - Defensible court or porch in front of an entrance. BARMKIN - Small defensible court adjoining a tower house. BARTIZAN - A turret corbelled out at the top of a wall, often at a corner. BASTION - A projection no higher than the curtain wall. BASTLE -Small defensible house containing a single living room over a byre for cattle. CORBEL - A projecting bracket supporting other stonework or timbers. CURTAIN WALL - A high enclosing wall around a bailey. EMBATTLED - provided with a parapet with indentations (crenellations). JAMB - A side of a doorway, window or other opening. KEEP - A citadel or ultimate strongpoint LIGHT - A compartment of a window. LOOP - A small opening to admit light or for the discharge of missiles. MACHICOLATION -A slot for dropping or firing missiles at assailants. MOAT - a defensive ditch, water filled or dry. MOTTE - A steep sided flat-topped mound, partly or wholly man-made. ORIEL - A bow window projecting out from just the upper part of a wall. PARAPET - A wall for protection at any sudden drop. PELE or PEEL - Originally a palisaded court, later coming to mean a bastle or tower house. PLINTH - The projecting base of a wall. PORTCULLIS - A wooden gate made to rise and fall in vertical grooves. POSTERN - A back entrance or lesser gateway. SOLAR - A private living room for the lord and his family. STRONGHOUSE - Dwelling made difficult to break into but not equipped for an active defence against a sustained or determined attack. TOWER HOUSE - Self contained defensible house with the rooms stacked vertically. WALL-WALK - A walkway on top of a wall, always protected by a parapet on at least one side. WARD - Stone walled defensive enclosure.

PUBLIC ACCESS TO THE SITES   Codes used in the gazetteer.

E Buildings in the care of English Heritage where an admission fee is payable.
F Buildings or sites to which there is free access at any reasonable time.
H Buildings currently used as hotels, restaurants, shops, etc.
O Buildings opened to the public by private owners, local councils, etc.
V Buildings closely visible from public roads, paths, churchyards & open spaces.

FURTHER READING

Norman Castles in Britain, Derek Renn, 1968.
Castles of Northumbria, Mike Jackson, 1992.
Castles of Durham and Cleveland, Mike Jackson, 1996.
Castellarium Anglicanum, DJ Cathcart-King, 2 vols, 1983
Victoria County History of Durham, three vols 1905-28.
Historic Sites of County Durham, Glyn Lyndon Dodds, 1996
Castles and Towers of County Durham, Robert Hugill, 1979
Historic Sites of County Durham, Glen Lyndon Dodds, 1996.
Durham volume of the Buildings of England series, Pevsner and Williamson, 1983
See articles (especially those by Peter Ryder) in Archeologia Aeliana, Durham
    Archeological Journal, Weardale Naturalists Field Club Journal, etc.
See also Medieval Archeology, Archeological Journal, and Country Life.
Guide books or histories are available for: Barnard, Durham, Hylton and Raby.
See also monographs by Peter Ryder on Old Hall Farm at High Coniscliffe,
    Ravensworth Castle, Walworth Castle, Witton Tower and Bastles in Weardale.